MW01254618

It's Not Their Business

A Self-Help Vision Journal by

Shani P. Nelson

ISBN: 9781097487042

It's Not Their Business vision journal is dedicated to all dreamers, creators, and entrepreneurs who refuse to settle no matter what. Your dreams are closer than you think.

To my children, Kendon, Jalia, and my future babies, I dedicate this vision journal to you as well. Your dreams will never be too far from your reach. I love y'all!

IT'S NOT THEIR BUSINESS VISION JOURNAL

ACKNOWLEDGMENTS

All honor and glory to God for using me in this way. Thank you for making sure I kept my dreams and sanity intact in spite of all the world has tried to throw at me.

Thank you to my husband who has always supported me.

Thank you for not allowing me to give up. Thank you Destined Eloquence Publishing, LLC for ALL you've done. Remember the promise because it shall be.

Thanks to all of my family, friends, and supporters. You all are everything to me!

Trust in the Lord with all your heart
and lean not on your own understanding;
in all your ways submit to him,
and he will make your paths straight.
Proverbs 5:6 NIV

Hey ________________________________!
(Insert your name here)

By picking up this journal, you are making a decision which can change your life forever. From this point on, your perspective determines the outcome of everything. Your attitude must shift into a positive gear that refuses to give up no matter what. Your glass should always be viewed as half-full instead of half-empty. You should always believe a way can be made. This journal is designed to impact your thinking. Your perspective of life and your destiny is about to change, but you must first make a decision. Decide that you'll be open to change in your thinking, attitude, and your expectations. Change must take place for new things to occur. Aren't you tired of the way things are going? Isn't that the reason you've opened this journal?

I'm Shani P. Nelson, and I've been there.

I've always been a dreamer. A dreamer of finding love, a dreamer of having a great family, a dreamer of having the perfect career, a dreamer of being a boss, a dreamer of having financial freedom, and a dreamer of working alongside the people who've inspired me the most. I believe with all my heart that all I've ever dreamed is going to happen because I'm setting goals and using my creativity to achieve greatness. Being creative has always been my outlet, but it hasn't always been an easy outlet to execute in successfully.

My 29 years of life has been filled with struggles. Abuse, depression, and anxiety are just a few of the battles that tried to take my dreams from me. I was blessed to have both of my parents as great providers, but I wasn't afforded the opportunities to hone my creativity. I would have loved to have my writing and musical ability perfected earlier on in life with professional help, but maybe they just didn't know how to accommodate my big dreams. Regardless of my feelings, I've never faulted my parents for anything in my life.

Although we may desire guidance prior to going into a journey, I've learned having to build our dreams from the bottom brings about a different type of satisfaction. Don't despise where you've been prior to this moment. I wasted a lot of time searching for the right doors and the right people who would help me to become a professional creator. As time passed and stagnation set in, I started to believe my creative abilities were just hobbies, instead of gifts I'm called to serve in. My passion for writing and music began to dwindle. My work ethic started to fade. I had a serious case of the "I don't wants." And then, I started feeding myself lies, making myself believe I wasn't good enough to achieve my aspirations of becoming a world-renown writer, influencer, and creator. I believed my dreams were moving further and further away from me each time an attempt to achieve a goal in my creativity failed. I grew to be dissatisfied with myself, and those negative effects began spilling on everyone around me. I pondered on all the negative aspects of my life and felt that I was stuck.

That was the lowest point of my life. For a creative, low points can either bury you or catapult you. I realized I could either bury myself in sorrow, or I could allow what I was going through to catapult me into my destiny. I decided I couldn't remain in that state of mind. Being able to express my creativity is my peace and I wanted that again.

I began to think about my life differently and I found the beauty in what God was doing in that season of my life. I've always thought lack of support for my creativity was a hindrance to being able to achieve my goals, but when I began to look at my goals as being attainable without the support, I realized their lack of support created a relentless ambition in me. No matter what situation arose, I've never given up on my goals. There were times I wanted nothing more than to throw in the towel. But God didn't allow me to give up on myself.

God kept reminding me of my progress. He allowed me to see just how far he had taken me already and He assured me He would take me much further along according to His promises. He reminded me that I should expect greatness to come from Him. Remembering His promises was all the fuel I needed to keep pressing on when everything around me seemed to be falling apart.

When I stopped playing the blame game and understood rejection was just God's way of showing me that He had better for me, my eyes opened even more. I could see myself clearer. I could see the greatness inside of me that God kept trying to convince me of. Oftentimes, we beat ourselves up over not being as far along in life as we believe we should be. You must learn to completely silence the doubt and negativity to look at where you are now. Think of your current situation and state of being as if you are exactly where you need to be for something amazing to happen for you.

Before you get started on your journey, I would like for you to take this time to fully forgive yourself. Forgive yourself for all the doubts you fed yourself, the times you believed you wasted your time, and any other negativity you've fed yourself. Cry it out if you must. Now, LET'S MOVE FORWARD!

Today, I'm asking you to dream again. Dream BIG! Nothing is impossible with God. Believe this with all your heart. When we're achieving our goals, we want those around us to be happy for us and support us, but you must understand even friends and family can hinder your success if you let them. Words of negativity and their absence could bring you to a halt. Many times, it's just their fears and lack of confidence they're trying to place on you. Don't take it personal. Just see it for what it is and continue to climb. This is the reason it's important to keep your ideas between you and God while it's in the birthing process. I know when these ideas and dreams come to you, you are so excited and you want to share it with everyone you know, but this could cause you more harm than you bargained for. So, I've created this journal for you to write the vision and make it plain. Remember, all you establish upon the Lord will come to pass. I pray this vision journal help you to see the goodness God planted on the inside of you and further understand your predestined purpose. Don't hold back! Be as personal and transparent as you can be. Don't be afraid to believe God for the impossible because if it is in His will, He will never let you down. Be willing to see who you truly are through the eyes of God. Get ready to live a life of peace, self-love, confidence, and prosperity. ***Pray and EXPECT!***

Habakkuk 2:2-3 KJV reads, *"And the Lord answered*

me, and said, "Write the vision, and make it plain upon tables, that he may run that readeth it. For the vision is yet for an appointed time, but at the end it shall speak, and not lie: though it tarry, wait for it; because it will surely come, it will not tarry."

As you journey through the phases of ***It's Not Their Business***, I implore you to incorporate prayer into every decision you make and in everything you do. Conversations with The One who created your destiny will make this journey a lot easier. Tell God everything that is on your heart and mind, then take the time to hear from God. He will tell you when this is the way and to walk in it (Isaiah 30:21 KJV). If you feel you have a hard time talking to God, no worries! I will help you pray through this. You are well on your way to living the life that you've dreamed of.

Dear Heavenly Father,

Thank You for all You have been to me thus far. I praise You because You are so good to me. Thank You for forgiving me and keeping me. Thank You for allowing me to align with my faith and begin the journey of seeking the person You've always planned for me to be. I'm excited Father God, and I believe from this point on, anything is possible. May my gifts bring me before the great. I plead the blood of Jesus over my journey and ask for Your will to be done.

In Jesus Name,
Amen.

Phase 1 :

THE END OF THE ROAD OR THE BEGINNING OF A NEW JOURNEY? YOU DECIDE.

Jeremiah 29:11 NIV reads,
"For I know the plans I have for you," declares the LORD, "plans to prosper you and not to harm you, plans to give you hope and a future."

»

Imagine completing high school in the top 10 of your class, getting accepted into a prestigious college, and getting super close to your junior year of college only to drop out because you have no clue of the direction your life is taking. This is what happened to me. I graduated fourth in my high school graduating class, enrolled in Louisiana State University, and fell flat on my face two years later.

I enrolled in college with a goal to pursue law school after graduation. I had a set path for what I wanted to do with my life. I thought my plan was set until what I thought I wanted didn't feel like it was meant to be anymore. I tried as best as I could to hold on to my plans because it pleased others, which is a common mistake we all make in our life's journey. We tend to care greatly about what make others happy rather than our own happiness, stifling our ability to be honest about what we truly desire. We must be careful about pleasing others and be intentional about our leadership in our life, as well as our originality.

My parents believed college would provide me with the foundation I needed to be successful in life, so I aspired to make my parents proud of me with my educational goals. With graduating fourth in my class and getting admitted into a prestigious university, I knew I was well on my way…until I became pregnant in the middle of my college career. A baby wasn't in my plans, but neither was disappointing my parents, so I made the best of my new situation. Dropping out of college was not an option, so I had to figure out my next move.

My son was scheduled to be born during the Christmas holiday break on December 16th by cesarean section. I figured I'd be well enough to return to school in time for the new semester, so I did. My new school routine began with leaving my son with family to take the daily hour drive to Baton Rouge. I was determined to accomplish my goal to show my parents that I could still make them proud. This new routine became overwhelming and I soon found myself pursuing a degree I no longer was interested in. My ambition for success kept me going, but I didn't know exactly where I was going anymore.

I've always known I wouldn't be a mediocre person. I just didn't know how I was going to get to my destined place.

I want you to be able to get to that destined place

without wasting time by living the life others want you to live. Don't worry about what others think because people will talk about you whether you are doing bad or good. So, you might as well do what you truly desire to do. It is important for you not to worry about the opinions people have of you and your dreams. What God put in you wasn't placed in you for others to understand. Learn to block out the noise of the world and focus on your inner passions. Commune with the Creator and find your purpose. Yes, your life has an amazing purpose, regardless of what your current circumstances may seem to be. Everyday won't be an easy day for you, but God wants us to enjoy the plans He has prepared for us. We weren't placed on Earth just to work, get a paycheck, pay bills, and pass on. In fact, Jesus said, *"I came that they may have life, and that they may have it more abundantly"* (John 10:10 KJV).

The following pages of this journal is meant for you to be honest with yourself. Remove the limits you've placed over your life and dig deep within. Pray about your answers and allow God to help you determine what He has placed inside of you. All the plans God has for you are only to prosper you and give you a future. Trust the Master's plan.

What are your hobbies and talents?

What are you good at doing which could possibly turn into a career?

What is your dream job?

Dear Heavenly Father,

Thank You for opening my eyes to my purpose. I thank You for showing me that I really can do anything with You by my side. God, I don't want to worry in this season. You've showed me so many great things that I can achieve, and I believe You have fully equipped me to do every good work. I am committing my dreams and aspirations to You. I know with them being in Your hands, prosperity is inevitable. Lead the way, God.

In Jesus Name,
Amen.

Phase 2:

IF YOU DON'T SPEAK IT, YOU DON'T WANT IT

Mark 11:24 NIV reads,
"Therefore I tell you, whatever you ask for in prayer, believe that you have received it, and it will be yours."

»

Now, let's write the vision and make it plain! The following space is being provided for your vision board. Place pictures, scriptures, phrases, lyrics, and anything else that'll serve as a reminder of your goals. This space should be created in a way to be a constant motivation for you to remain aligned with the plans God has for you. Remember to take the limits off and believe. Anything is possible with God. ***Pray and EXPECT!***

Dear Heavenly Father,

Thank You for showing me the vision of what life could be. I praise You for taking me out of the box I once was in. Thank You for blessing me with my gifts, talents, and abilities. I dedicate them back to You. Do whatever You please with them. I know they will only bring me to Your glory. I trust You with my life. May Your will be done in my life.

In Jesus Name,
Amen.

Circle Assessment

Now that you have begun to explore the endless possibilities of who you can be, I'd like you to take note of a very influential aspect of this process. Who is in your circle? Who is apart of your support system? It is crucial for you to be surrounded by people who are genuinely for you. The people you surround yourself with doesn't have to understand your vision now, but they must believe in you. Don't let people who don't believe in you get too close to you. The harsh reality of evaluating your circle is that some of the people you need to distance yourself from can very well be a family member or even your best friend. It can sometimes be a hard pill to swallow, but assessing your circle is one of the most important decisions you must make when you're chasing after your destiny.

Make sure your circle is motivating you. Encouraging words are great to hear, but it's so much more that's needed. The people in your circle need to believe in you enough to hold you accountable. If you begin to show any sign of slacking, you need to trust that they will remind you of the reason you are doing whatever you have started. They need to push you to get back on track. Your circle must also believe in something for themselves as well. Just as they are holding you accountable for your life, they should be committed to living a progressive life as well. Keep ambitious and diligent people in your midst. The right circle will keep you moving forward when the journey gets tough. You'll always have the mindset of goal-reaching when you are around people who are constantly attaining their goals.

My circle consists of ambitious women who are college graduates, career-driven, homeowners, entrepreneurs, and corporate professionals. The women in my circle are women who exudes excellence. They have been great examples of motivation during my low moments on this journey. Although it may have taken me a little more time to achieve some of my goals, no one in my circle has made me feel inferior, even when they may have not understood my path. Your circle must keep you uplifted and encouraged. Their presence in your life should push you to excel. No one in your circle should make you doubt yourself or drown you in negativity.

Dead weight (people who aren't contributing anything to your success but are constantly taking from you) can only slow you down. If you aren't careful, you could end up being surrounded by people who only want to use you. Watch out for jealousy and anyone who leads you to be unproductive. Don't take their negativity personally. Most of the time, people aren't mad about what you are doing, they are mad because they can't do what you are doing. You are going to have to pray for discernment and master the art of distancing yourself from people, places, and things that move you away from our goals.

Dear Heavenly Father,

Thank You for keeping my heart safe. I praise You for always having my best interest in mind. You know the hearts of all the people in my life. You know who is good for me and who is not. Father give me discernment to know who me should be around and give me the strength to disconnect from those who shouldn't. Please keep those around me who will help me carry the burden of my vision and those I can provide the same support for in return. Put me on the minds of the people who can further what I am doing in my life. Bring the right people to me. Build me the perfect support system and if that system only includes You, teach me to embrace this season with all that I am. Help me learn to be quick to forgive.

In Jesus Name,
Amen.

Phase 3:

TO WHOM MUCH IS GIVEN, MUCH IS REQUIRED

Philippians 2:5-7 NIV reads,
"In your relationships with one another, have the same mindset as Christ Jesus: Who, being in very nature, God, did not consider equality with God something to be used to His own advantage; rather, He made himself nothing by taking the very nature of a servant, being made in human likeness."

»

As contrary as it may sound, there is freedom in serving. For you to live your dreams and have financial freedom, you must first be willing to serve your fellow man. You bring what you have to offer to the table with the intent of using it to help someone else. We must adopt a lifestyle of service to bloom into its greatest level of freedom. I'm not sure where you are spiritually, but I'd like to share an example that has always helped me view servanthood in a clearer perspective. The life of Jesus is the most successful example of service and freedom. I've learned that I'm guaranteed a life free of bondage just by adopting the attitude of Christ in every aspect of my life.

Jesus was the very nature of God, but He didn't view himself as equal. No matter what our position in life may be, Jesus taught us that serving others should be amongst our first intentions. We must not focus on selfish gain; Humility should be our foundational purpose.

Jesus lived a life of service, giving of Himself to all those in need without feeling entitled or looking to be served in return. Jesus made Himself relatable with his humanlikeness, understanding our human struggles mentally and in physicality. This made Him a perfect candidate to supply all our needs. Like Jesus, we need to be able to know what the people need and give to them through our services. As we supply the needs of others, God supplies our needs and brings overflow to us. You'd be blessing someone with your gift and reaping financial freedom at the same time. *"For you were called to freedom, brothers. Only do not use your freedom as an opportunity for the flesh, but through love serve one another"* (Galatians 5:13 ESV).

What are your gifts?

What services can you provide to help others?

What makes you stand out from the rest?

Dear Heavenly Father,

Thank You for being a great example of servanthood. I praise You for showing me how it's supposed to be done. You also give me grace and show me mercy when I am unable to match up with Your model. Father, I ask You to give me a servant's heart. I am willing to use the gifts You have given me to help others. Show me how to be selfless and give of myself more. Even when I don't understand or when my emotions try to hinder me, I ask You quicken my spirit. I want to be like You.

In Jesus Name,
Amen.

Phase 4:

YOU ALREADY HAVE THE TOOLS! NOW, GET TO WORK!

Hebrews 13:20-21 NIV reads,
"Now may the God of peace, who through the blood of the eternal covenant brought back from the dead our Lord Jesus, that great Shepherd of the sheep, equip you with everything good for doing his will, and may he work in us what is pleasing to him, through Jesus Christ, to whom be glory for ever and ever. Amen."

»

There may be moments along your journey when you may feel alone. In those moments, remember God is with you and He is the ultimate source for you to continue on. If you don't have a relationship with God, or if you've become distant in your faith, I encourage you to renew your relationship with God. In His light is where your success awaits. God is a present help (Psalm 46:1 NIV), a provider (Psalm 145:16 NIV), and a way-maker (Isaiah 43:19 NIV). The most amazing news about this truth is that God placed the same kind of power He gave Jesus to succeed within us!

He has also graced us with the power to ask for the things we may not currently have (Philippians 4:19 KJV). God has fully equipped us to do great works (Hebrews 13:20-21 ESV). We must believe. Your faith is what drives your ambitions and pushes you to be who you dream to be (Proverbs 23:7). Putting good energy into the atmosphere through prayer, positive thoughts, and speaking yourself into greatness creates opportunities for you. We must believe we can get what we need. Strive with all your heart and God will be sure to enhance you.

We must learn to follow God's leading when it comes to recognizing and properly using our resources. Don't be fooled. The enemy sees your potential as well and will try to do everything in his power to prevent the plan of God from going forth. There may be people and opportunities that may come available which appear to be open doors that'll propel you to the next level, but all opportunities are not good opportunities. Some opportunities may be a hindrance to your path. Seek God, hear His voice, and be mindful of the decisions you make during this phase. Be mindful of the people who come around offering their help. There will be people who want to help you just so they can say they did. There will be people who want to help you just to control you. This is the reason God will often have you walk out your visions with only Him at your side. We must focus on the strategy God gives us to achieve our goals. The challenge is in listening to God when He reveal the suitable people who is in His will for our lives. Let's create a checklist of all the things you will need to move forward in your goals.

- [ ] ______________________________
- [ ] ______________________________
- [ ] ______________________________
- [ ] ______________________________
- [ ] ______________________________
- [ ] ______________________________
- [ ] ______________________________
- [ ] ______________________________
- [ ] ______________________________
- [ ] ______________________________
- [ ] ______________________________
- [ ] ______________________________
- [ ] ______________________________
- [ ] ______________________________
- [ ] ______________________________
- [ ] ______________________________
- [ ] ______________________________

Dear Heavenly Father,

Thank You for all the provisions You've given me thus far. I praise You because You are my source. You make all things happen for me. You are my way-maker and provider. I pray You bring me all I need to further my visions and further my personal growth. I pray You block all the schemes and plans of the enemy. Always keep me in position. No matter what comes along this journey, I may never forget You are the Ultimate Source.

In Jesus Name,
Amen.

Phase 5:

FEARS & SOLUTIONS

2 Timothy 1:7 NLT NIV reads,
"For God has not given us a spirit of fear and timidity, but of power, love, and self-discipline."

»

When you have a dream that is bigger than your present reality, fear always tries to creep in and stop you. People often fear the process because of the highs and lows that are attached to accomplishments. Prepare yourself for rejection, negativity, to lose relationships, and many other situations that may arise. Don't allow fear of the unknown to overwhelm you. Instead, be encouraged with knowing God is bigger than any problem. He has anointed you for a purpose.

When I decided I was going to pursue a career in entertainment, instead of pursuing a career in the law field, I became fearful. I knew it'd be a scary journey to take, but the risk would be worth it because everything would lead to a career I was born to be in. I knew I'd be risking the "guarantee of a successful life" that I always said I'd have. I would also be risking a lot of my time. Individuals who pursue careers in entertainment may end up spending many years just trying to become relevant. Sometimes they may never get there at all. I would no longer have the security of obtaining a degree in a field where a job would always be available for me, I would now have to create my own opportunities to secure my finances. Evaluating all the aspects of the entertainment industry didn't make my fears any lighter, either. I would now be entering a career field that is known to have demonic influences, but here is where being a believer in God put me in the lead. I decided I would go into the industry as His light, shining in the darkness. I figured out the solutions to two of my fears. But, then came the fear of success. Yes, there is such a thing as being afraid of success.

You don't know how life will change once you achieve all the goals you've been striving for. When I wasn't so sure of myself, I feared getting into the industry and losing my salvation. I thought I would get caught up with wanting to be "down." I feared success would be too much for me to handle. I feared my attitude at that time would cause me to make major mistakes due to lack of self-control. Constantly being scrutinized and sometimes mentally maimed by the world can cause a person's character to negatively shift. At one point I was adamant about "taking care" of all the people who tried to play me. I was looking back at all the people who didn't believe in me. I wanted to make them regret not helping me. Then there were sometimes when I feared I wasn't good enough. It's so easy to compare yourself to your peers and find every flaw you could possibly have. Refrain from doing that.

Eventually, fear consumed me and forced me to become stagnant. I couldn't create music or write stories and it was all because of negative thoughts. Fear is merely an illusion we form in our minds when we <u>think</u> something is scary. It's an emotion that grows within us when we are afraid of change. Feelings are fickle and are controlled by you. I wasted valuable time that could have been spent working towards my career, thinking of all that could go wrong. I don't want this to happen to you. If it has been happening, make the choice now to silence your fears. Dig deep and confess them here.

Get in a place where you can sit quietly and really rummage through your mind. Close your eyes and breathe deeply. Walk with confidence into the spaces of your mind you tried to avoid and identify your fears. Be completely honest with yourself because the things you are afraid of are the things that is holding you back. It's time to break free. Once you've identified them, write them down.

Fear will use any vehicle it can to get into your mind. The fear of failure is the most common mechanism used. Let me let you in on something. You are going to fail repeatedly along this journey. You may get a bunch of rejections before you get an approval, but you must keep going. Always return to the drawing board to re-strategize. God will continue to elevate you.

Now that you've confronted your fears, keep them far away! I suggest you pray. You can get all your strength back after a conversation with God, the One who created the passion within you. Trust that God has gone ahead of you and paved the way for you! The enemy knows the moment God gets you past this mind hurdle, there is no stopping you. Decree and declare that you will no longer allow fear to keep you bound. Love your vision enough to not let fear hinder you from achieving your best. God is with you! *"Have I not commanded you? Be strong and courageous. Do not be afraid; do not be discouraged, for the LORD your God will be with you wherever you go"* (Joshua 1:9).

Write a letter or a declaration to yourself about conquering your fears. What will you do every day to keep your mind clear and focused?

Dear Heavenly Father,

Thank You for showing me who I am. I praise You because You have not given me a spirit of fear. Today, I declare I will no longer identify with it. Forgive me for being too afraid to move before now. I decree and declare that I will never go back to that way of thinking. I thank You for a sound mind and the courage to continue on. You are for me, so I don't care who is against me. I am victorious in Jesus Name.

Amen.

Phase 6:

FURTHER THAN THAT

Romans 8:28 NIV reads,
"And we know that in all things God works for the good of those who love him, who have been called according to his purpose."

»

God's plans for us always goes far beyond what we plan for ourselves. However, He does care about giving us our heart's desires when we delight ourselves in Him. Though God has the final say, I believe He takes our desires into consideration. He wants us to have His best and He has the power to make our desires pure enough to attain just that. So, dream out loud without any limitations on what you want and who you can been. You can do anything you put your mind to. You must trust God and believe in yourself. As we get closer to the part of the journey where we must begin to add action to our faith, I'd like you to think about where in God's best do you see yourself in 5 years. Where do you want to live? Would you like to be married? Would you like to start a family? What would be your career? What steps do you plan on taking to make this a reality? Use this worksheet to sketch out your very own 5-year plan. When you know exactly what you want in life, it's easier to map out a path. Identify the most important items on each list and then place them in the year that you'd like to achieve them. *"For I know the plans I have for you," declares the LORD, "plans to prosper you and not to harm you, plans to give you hope and a future"* (Jeremiah 29:11).

5-Year Plan

Describe what your life was like 5 years ago.

What would you like to change about your life today?

Envision your life in 5 years. Be specific. List 3 steps you're going to take to achieve each goal and attach a date to each goal.

What do you believe you were called to do in life?

Are you fulfilling your purpose? If not, what's holding you back?

What does success look like in your eyes?

What motivates you to accomplish your goals?

How do you handle setbacks and disappointments? What can you do to better improve your response?

____

____

____

____

____

____

____

____

____

Name a few challenges you've overcome. Describe the process you took to gain victory over the struggle.

____

____

____

____

____

____

List your weaknesses and ways you can overcome them.

____

____

____

____

____

____

____

____

Is there anything you'd like to change about yourself? If so, what is it?

____

____

____

____

____

____

____

____

How will achieving my goal help the people I love?

Dear Heavenly Father,

Thank You for getting me to the point of organizing my life. I praise You because You are worthy and capable of bringing everything I declare to pass. Your power is unmatched, and your wisdom is undefeatable. God, I want to delight myself in You. May my heart's desires always align with Your will for my life. God guide me in the way I should go and help me to see what You've already planned. Help me to have the right goals and know where to place them in this 5-year plan. I trust Your guidance.

In Jesus Name,
Amen.

Phase 7:

NOW, IT'S TIME TO DO WORK! WEEKLY GOALS & TO DO LISTS

Psalm 37:4 NIV reads,
"Take delight in the Lord,
and he will give you the desires of your heart.

»

LIGHTS! CAMERA! ACTION!! You've taken one of the largest leaps of faith by going through these phases to discover your great purpose. The life you want to live is right in front of you. Don't think about the amount of time it will take. Don't think about what you're missing. Just think about putting things into action. Understand your dream won't happen overnight, but the more steps you take, the closer you'll get to it. Also understand that every attempt won't be successful, but it'll be a learning experience. It's all about how you view your process. Faith without works is dead, so it's time to set goals and meet them. Be realistic with these goals. Make sure they can be achieved. Nothing is ever too small when it comes to taking steps so write it all down. Be intentional with your moves. The ultimate goal is to get to the destination God has ordained for you. Use the following 30 worksheets to set your daily and weekly goals and 'To Do Lists'. This will help to keep you focused. It'll also be there for you to fall back on when you get distracted because we know life is full of distractions. Do your very best to stay on task and believe. "In the same way, faith by itself, if it is not accompanied by action, is dead" (James 2:17).

Dear Heavenly Father,

Thank You for placing Your spirit in me. I praise You because You are mighty and strong. God, please keep me diligent. If I ever get distracted, God, please nudge me to get on task. Help me to make realistic goals and fill me with Your guidance to meet them. I believe You have ordained me for greatness, and I am ready to walk in it.

In Jesus Name,
Amen.

Goal:______________________________________

Date:______________________________________

Accomplish Date:____________________________

To Do List:

Goal:____________________________________

Date:____________________________________

Accomplish Date:__________________________

To Do List:

Goal:______________________________________

Date:______________________________________

Accomplish Date:___________________________

To Do List:

Goal:____________________________________

Date:____________________________________

Accomplish Date:__________________________

To Do List:

Goal:____________________________________

Date:____________________________________

Accomplish Date:__________________________

To Do List:

Goal:__________________________________

Date:__________________________________

Accomplish Date:__________________________

To Do List:

Goal:__________________________________

Date:__________________________________

Accomplish Date:_________________________

To Do List:

Goal:____________________________________

Date:____________________________________

Accomplish Date:__________________________

To Do List:

Goal:____________________________________

Date:____________________________________

Accomplish Date:__________________________

To Do List:

Goal:____________________________________

Date:____________________________________

Accomplish Date:__________________________

To Do List:

Goal:________________________________

Date:________________________________

Accomplish Date:_______________________

To Do List:

Goal:____________________________________

Date:____________________________________

Accomplish Date:__________________________

To Do List:

Goal:____________________________________

Date:____________________________________

Accomplish Date:__________________________

To Do List:

Goal:____________________________________

Date:____________________________________

Accomplish Date:__________________________

To Do List:

Goal:________________________________

Date:________________________________

Accomplish Date:________________________

To Do List:

Goal:______________________________________

Date:______________________________________

Accomplish Date:____________________________

To Do List:

Goal:________________________________

Date:________________________________

Accomplish Date:_______________________

To Do List:

Goal:____________________________________

Date:____________________________________

Accomplish Date:__________________________

To Do List:

Goal:____________________________________

Date:____________________________________

Accomplish Date:__________________________

To Do List:

Goal:____________________________________

Date:____________________________________

Accomplish Date:____________________________

To Do List:

Goal:____________________________________

Date:____________________________________

Accomplish Date:__________________________

To Do List:

Goal:__________________________________

Date:__________________________________

Accomplish Date:_________________________

To Do List:

Goal:______________________________________

Date:______________________________________

Accomplish Date:____________________________

To Do List:

Goal:____________________________________

Date:____________________________________

Accomplish Date:__________________________

To Do List:

Goal:____________________________________

Date:____________________________________

Accomplish Date:__________________________

To Do List:

Goal:______________________________________

Date:______________________________________

Accomplish Date:____________________________

To Do List:

Goal:____________________________________

Date:____________________________________

Accomplish Date:__________________________

To Do List:

Goal:____________________________________

Date:____________________________________

Accomplish Date:__________________________

To Do List:

Goal:____________________________________

Date:____________________________________

Accomplish Date:__________________________

To Do List:

Goal:__________________________________

Date:__________________________________

Accomplish Date:_________________________

To Do List:

Goal:____________________________________

Date:____________________________________

Accomplish Date:__________________________

To Do List:

CONGRATULATIONS!

You've completed a huge step on a journey that many don't have the courage to plan. I pray this journal keeps you inspired, encouraged, and diligent. Don't see this process as a selfish gesture because you've decided to confide in this journal instead of your loved ones. Don't get me wrong. There is nothing wrong with discussing your goals with a trusted individual. If you do choose to share with someone, I suggest you confide in someone who would be willing to hold you accountable. Try your hardest to surround yourself with positive vibes and optimism. The journey is hard enough by itself. Negative energy will only make it even harder. Our Father God operates in excellence and we have His spirit. It's only right for us to chase greatness for His glory. We are the light and people should see God in us. How can our light shine if we aren't walking in success? That's what this is all about! People will look at our lives and want to know who our God is. As life gets better, your success grows, and your blessings become even more abundant, you must remain humble. Nothing will last outside of God. The only reason we arrive at our destination is because of God's guidance. He'll make a way for us to fulfill our purpose. We must never forget that our gifts aren't just our gifts. We should do what we do with the intent of being a blessing to others. If you think with that kind of mentality, you'll always be prosperous. Don't stop dreaming! In all things, be thankful and show your gratitude by helping others. Commune with God and get your plan in order. Make sure you know exactly what you want to do before you start letting people in on what you are doing. It is better to have your project or goal completed before you say a word to anyone. Don't give anyone the opportunity to fill your mind with negative thoughts that may make you draw back from pursuing your dreams. Write out your vision, gather all your resources, and then make it happen.

Until then, ***It's Not Their Business.***

Love Always,
Shani P. Nelson

DECLARATIONS, AFFIRMATIONS, & PRAYERS FOR YOUR JOURNEY

SPEAK AND THINK LIFE

Now that you have identified your talents and your God-given vision is on its way to fruition, there is something I'd like for you to keep in mind. The outcome of this journey is going to greatly rely on what you speak and think. Think about how life was for you before you began this journey. Can you recall the way you spoke about yourself and your dreams? When was the last time you spoke positively about yourself and your situation? As a believer in Christ, the ability to decree a thing and it be established is a guaranteed possibility (Job 22:28)! Speak life over your dreams, your tasks, and yourself. Be optimistic when working on your goals. Never state that the task at hand is too hard. Instead, declare that you'll conquer it. Your words have power. We should always think before speaking because everything begins in our mind.

Renewing your mind and speaking positively is a choice you must consciously make daily. By transforming your speech to be aligned with God's Word, you'll become aligned with Him and who He has called you to be. Use your thoughts and your words to attract what you want.

You must have the right type of attitude to shape your mind in a way that would bring about success.

Think of how you view yourself and your life. Have you put limitations on yourself? Have you truly allowed yourself to think of more ways of how you can win? Or, are you too busy in thought of where you come from to think about the great places you can go? You can't doubt your capabilities because of your surroundings, the people who've failed before you, or even your insecurities. The Word says you can do **ALL** things through Christ (Philippians 4:13). You must believe in your mind that God is able to give you the desires of your heart. Let go of anything that doesn't progress you.

I have provided a list of affirmations, prayers, and scriptures to help you along your journey. Be Blessed! Be Encouraged! Just BE!

"A gift opens the way and ushers the giver into the presence of the great." (Proverbs 18:16 NIV)

Dear Heavenly Father,

Thank You for Your Word. I praise You because You always know exactly what needs to be said. Father, forgive me for every idle word I have spoken and help me to only speak the right things from now on. I speak life over each vision and dream You have given me. I speak life over myself. Lord, please help me make my thoughts remain submitted to You and Your purpose for my life. I rebuke a vain imagination and I welcome good thoughts. Lord, help me to think and speak prosperity from here on out.

In Jesus Name,
Amen.

AFFIRM YOURSELF AND YOUR SITUATIONS

I am enough.

I am completely confident in myself.

I am able because God has made me able.

I am strong enough to persevere.

I am a finisher.

I am courageous.

I am the one they've been waiting for.

I learn from my mistakes.

I know I can accomplish anything I set my mind to.

I forgive myself for not being perfect.

I will never give up.

I accept what I cannot change.

I make the best of every situation.

I'll find ways to laugh at things even when it's hard.

I can achieve anything because anything is possible.

I enjoy life to the fullest.

I have complete control over my thoughts, feelings, and

actions.

I stand for what I believe and will not be shaken.

I accept others for who they are.

I contribute my talents and knowledge for the good of all.

I make a difference whenever I can.

I commit to learning new things.

I strive to be open-minded.

I live in the moment while learning from the past and preparing

for the future.

I am God's child.

I am the head and not the tail.

I am above and never beneath.

I am a great steward over the gifts I am given.

I commit to perfecting my craft.

I strive to be a listener.

WEALTH AFFIRMATIONS

I am a magnet for money.

Prosperity is drawn to me.

Money comes to me in expected and unexpected ways.

My thinking is being transformed from a poverty-ridden mindset to a mind full of abundant thoughts.

I am worthy of making more money.

I am open and receptive to all the wealth life offers me.

I embrace new avenues of income.

I welcome an unlimited source of income and wealth in my life.

I bind all negative energy over my money.

Money comes to me easily and effortlessly.

I use money to better my life and the lives of others.

Wealth constantly flows into my life.

My actions create constant prosperity.

I am aligned with the energy of abundance.

I constantly attract opportunities that create more

money.

Money is the root of joy and comfort.

Money and spirituality can co-exist in harmony.

Money and love can be friends.

Money is my servant.

I am the master of my wealth.

I can manage large sums of money.

I can handle massive success with grace.

Money expands my life's opportunities and experiences.

Money creates positive impact in my life.

SCRIPTURES TO HELP YOU ON YOUR JOURNEY

Diligence

"All hard work brings a profit, but mere talk leads only to poverty." (Proverbs 14:23 NIV)

"The soul of the sluggard craves and gets nothing, while the soul of the diligent is richly supplied." (Proverbs 13:4 ESV)

"And let us not grow weary of doing good, for in due season we will reap, if we do not give up." (Galatians 6:9 ESV)

"The hand of the diligent will rule, while the slothful will be put to forced labor." (Proverbs 12:24 ESV)

"The plans of the diligent lead surely to abundance, but everyone who is hasty comes to poverty." (Proverbs 21:5 ESV)

"Blessed is the man who remains steadfast under trial, for when he has stood the test he will receive the crown of life, which God has promised to those who love Him." (James 1:12 ESV)

"But since you excel in everything—in faith, in speech, in knowledge, in complete earnestness and in the love we have kindled in you — see that you also excel in this grace of giving." (2 Corinthians 8:7 NIV)

Doubt and Fear

"When I am afraid, I put my trust in you." (Psalm 56:3 NIV)

"Do not be anxious about anything, but in every situation, by prayer and petition, with thanksgiving, present your requests to God. And the peace of God, which transcends all understanding, will guard your hearts and your minds in Christ Jesus." (Philippians 4:6-7 NIV)

"Peace I leave with you; my peace I give you. I do not give to you as the world gives. Do not let your hearts be troubled and do not be afraid." (John 14:27 NIV)

"For God has not given us a spirit of fear, but of power and of love and of a sound mind." (2 Timothy 1:7 NKJV)

"When anxiety was great within me, your consolation brought me joy." (Psalm 94:19 NIV)

"Be strong and courageous. Do not be afraid or terrified because of them, for the Lord your God goes with you; He will never leave you nor forsake you." (Deuteronomy 31:6 NIV)

"'For I am the Lord, your God, who takes hold of your right hand and says to you, Do not fear; I will help you. Do not be afraid, for I myself will help you,' declares the Lord, your Redeemer, the Holy One of Israel." (Isaiah 41:13-14 NIV)

Encouragement

"But those who hope in the LORD will renew their strength. They will soar on wings like eagles; they will run and not grow weary, they will walk and not be faint.." (Isaiah 40:31 NIV)

"When you pass through the waters, I will be with you; and when you pass through the rivers, they will not sweep over you. When you walk through the fire, you will not be burned; the flames will not set you ablaze.." (Isaiah 43:2 NIV)

"Therefore, my dear brothers and sisters, stand firm. Let nothing move you. Always give yourselves fully to the work of the Lord, because you know that your labor in the Lord is not in vain." (1 Corinthians 15:58)

"The Lord himself goes before you and will be with you; he will never leave you nor forsake you. Do not be afraid; do not be discouraged." (Deuteronomy 31:8 NIV)

"Be strong and take heart, all you who hope in the Lord." (Psalm 31:24 NIV)

"I will instruct you and teach you in the way you should go; I will counsel you with my loving eye on you." (Psalm 32:8 NIV)

"Be on your guard; stand firm in the faith; be courageous; be strong." (1 Corinthians 16:13 NIV)

Faith

"Therefore I tell you, whatever you ask for in prayer, believe that you have received it, and it will be yours." (Mark 11:24 NIV)

"Now faith is confidence in what we hope for and assurance about what we do not see." (Hebrews 11:1 NIV)

"But when you ask, you must believe and not doubt, because the one who doubts is like a wave of the sea, blown and tossed by the wind." (James 1:6 NIV)

"Have faith in God," Jesus answered. "Truly I tell you, if anyone says to this mountain, 'Go, throw yourself into the sea,' and does not doubt in their heart but believes that what they say will happen, it will be done for them. Therefore I tell you, whatever you ask for in prayer, believe that you have received it, and it will be yours." (Mark 11:22-24 NIV)

"Now to him who is able to do far more abundantly than all that we ask or think, according to the power at work within us." (Ephesians 3:20 ESV)

"What then shall we say to these things? If God is for us, who can be against us?" (Romans 8:31 ESV)

"So do not fear, for I am with you; do not be dismayed, for I am your God. I will strengthen you and help you; I will uphold you with my righteous right hand.." (Isaiah 41:10 NIV)

Guidance

"Show me your ways, Lord, teach me your paths. Guide me in your truth and teach me, for you are God my Savior, and my hope is in you all day long." (Psalm 25:4-5 NIV)

"If any of you lacks wisdom, you should ask God, who gives generously to all without finding fault, and it will be given to you. But when you ask, you must believe and not doubt, because the one who doubts is like a wave of the sea, blown and tossed by the wind." (James 1:5-6 NIV)

"Lead me, Lord, in Your righteousness because of my enemies— make your way straight before me." (Psalm 5:8 NIV)

"Since You are my rock and my fortress, for the sake of Your name lead and guide me." (Psalm 31:3 NIV)

"Hear my cry, O God; listen to my prayer. From the ends of the earth I call to you, I call as my heart grows faint; lead me to the rock that is higher than I." (Psalm 61:1-2 NIV)

"Let the morning bring me word of your unfailing love, for I have put my trust in You. Show me the way I should go, for to You I entrust my life." (Psalm 143:8 NIV)

"I will praise the Lord, who counsels me; even at night my heart instructs me. I keep my eyes always on the Lord. With Him at my right hand, I will not be shaken." (Psalm 16:7-8 NIV)

Helping Others

"Do not neglect to do good and to share what you have, for such sacrifices are pleasing to God." (Hebrews 13:16 ESV)

"Let each of you look not only to his own interests, but also to the interests of others." (Philippians 2:4 ESV)

"Give, and it will be given to you. Good measure, pressed down, shaken together, running over, will be put into your lap. For with the measure you use it will be measured back to you." (Luke 6:38 ESV)

"But if anyone has the world's goods and sees his brother in need, yet closes his heart against him, how does God's love abide in him?" (1 John 3:17 ESV)

"Whoever is generous to the poor lends to the Lord, and he will repay him for his deed." (Proverbs 19:17 ESV)

"In the same way, let your light shine before others, so that they may see your good works and give glory to your Father who is in heaven." (Matthew 5:16 ESV)

"Give to the one who begs from you, and do not refuse the one who would borrow from you." (Matthew 5:42 ESV)

Humility

"Do nothing out of selfish ambition or vain conceit. Rather, in humility value others above yourselves." (Philippians 2:3 NIV)

"Live in harmony with one another. Do not be proud, but be willing to associate with people of low position. Do not be conceited." (Romans 12:16 NIV)

"Humble yourselves before the Lord, and He will lift you up." (James 4:10 NIV)

"Therefore, as God's chosen people, holy and dearly loved, clothe yourselves with compassion, kindness, humility, gentleness and patience." (Colossians 3:12 NIV)

"Humility is the fear of the Lord; its wages are riches and honor and life." (Proverbs 22:4 NIV)

"If my people, who are called by my name, will humble themselves and pray and seek my face and turn from their wicked ways, then I will hear from heaven, and I will forgive their sin and will heal their land." (2 Chronicles 7:14 NIV)

"Wisdom's instruction is to fear the Lord, and humility comes before honor." (Proverbs 15:33 NIV)

Overwhelmed

"From the end of the earth I call to you when my heart is faint. Lead me to the rock that is higher than I." (Psalm 61:2 NIV)

"When my spirit was overwhelmed within me, then thou knewest my path. In the way wherein I walked have they privily laid a snare for me.." (Psalm 142:3 KJV)

"Do not let your hearts be troubled. Trust in God; trust also in Me." (John 14:1 NIV)

"The LORD is my strength and my shield; my heart trusts in Him, and He helps me. My heart leaps for joy, and with my song I praise Him.." (Psalm 28:7 NIV)

"Commit your way to the LORD; trust in Him, and He will act." (Psalm 37:5 ESV)

"The steps of a man are established by the LORD, when he delights in his way." (Psalm 37:23 ESV)

"Finally, be strong in the Lord and in His mighty power." (Ephesians 6:10 NIV)

Purpose

"But I have raised you up for this very purpose, that I might show you my power and that my name might be proclaimed in all the earth." (Exodus 9:16 KJV)

"I know that you can do all things; no purpose of yours can be thwarted." (Job 42:2 NIV)

"The purposes of a person's heart are deep waters, but one who has insight draws them out." (Proverbs 20:5 NIV)

"Therefore, my dear friends, as you have always obeyed—not only in my presence, but now much more in my absence—continue to work out your salvation with fear and trembling, for it is God who works in you to will and to act in order to fulfill His good purpose." (Philippians 2:12-13)

"And we know that in all things God works for the good of those who love Him, who have been called according to His purpose." (Romans 8:28 NIV)

"He has saved us and called us to a holy life—not because of anything we have done but because of His own purpose and grace. This grace was given us in Christ Jesus before the beginning of time…" (2 Timothy 1:9 NIV)

Thankfulness

"It is good to give thanks to the Lord, and to sing praises to Your name, O Most High; To declare Your lovingkindness in the morning, And Your faithfulness every night,." (Psalm 92:1-2 NKJV)

"Continue earnestly in prayer, being vigilant in it with thanksgiving." (Colossians 4:2 NKJV)

"Whatever you do in word or deed, do all in the name of the Lord Jesus, giving thanks to God the Father through Him." (Colossians 3:17 ESV)

"Every good gift and every perfect gift is from above, coming down from the Father of lights with whom there is no variation or shadow due to change." (James 1:17 ESV)

"Oh give thanks to the LORD, call upon His name; Make known His deeds among the peoples!" (1 Chronicles 16:8 ESV)

"Therefore, since we receive a kingdom which cannot be shaken, let us show gratitude, by which we may offer to God acceptable worship, with reverence and awe." (Hebrews 12:28 ESV)

"Rejoice always, pray without ceasing, give thanks in all circumstances; for this is the will of God in Christ Jesus for you."
(1 Thessalonians 5:16-18 ESV)

Vision

"I can do all this through Him who gives me strength." (Philippians 4:13 NIV)

"Trust in the Lord with all your heart, and do not lean on your own understanding. In all your ways acknowledge him, and He will make straight your paths." (Proverbs 3:5-6 NIV)

"For God so loved the world, that He gave His only Son, that whoever believes in Him shall not perish but have eternal life." (John 3:16 NIV)

"Know therefore that the LORD your God is God; He is the faithful God who keeps covenant and steadfast love with those who love Him and keep His commandments." (Deuteronomy 7:9 NIV)

"As the Father has loved me, so have I loved you. Now remain in my love. If you keep my commands, you will remain in my love, just as I have kept my Father's commands and remain in His love. I have told you this so that my joy may be in you and that your joy may be complete. My command is this: Love each other as I have loved you. Greater love has no one than this: to lay down one's life for one's friends. You are my friends if you do what I command. I no longer call you servants, because a servant does not know his master's business. Instead, I have called you friends, for everything that I learned from my Father I have made known to you. You did not choose me, but I chose you and appointed you so that you might go and bear fruit—fruit that will last—and so that whatever you ask in my name the Father will give you. This is my command: Love each other." (John 15:9-17 NIV)

"No, in all these things we are more than conquerors through him who loved us. For I am convinced that neither death nor life, neither angels nor demons, neither the present nor the future, nor any powers, neither height nor depth, nor anything else in all creation, will be able to separate us from the love of God that is in Christ Jesus our Lord." (Romans 8:37-39 NIV)

"The Lord your God is with you, the Mighty Warrior who saves. He will take great delight in you; in His love He will no longer rebuke you, but will rejoice over you with singing." (Zephariah 3:17 NIV)

"Being confident of this very thing, that He which hath begun a good work in you will perform it until the day of Jesus Christ." (Philippians 1:6 KJV)

"No temptation has overtaken you that is not common to man. God is faithful, and he will not let you be tempted beyond your ability, but with the temptation he will also provide the way of escape, that you may be able to endure it." (1 Corinthians 10:13 NIV)

Made in the USA
Monee, IL
16 July 2020

36652568R00069